Praise for Jane Beal's
SONG OF THE SELKIE

***

The poems in *Song of the Selkie* take us deep into dream space. They explore archetypes that arise from the surging ocean of psyche and soul. Drawn from Nordic tales and the biblical story of Ruth, the woman who speaks in these pages speaks with pathos, desire, and knowing that come from the mystery, the "deep, deep Ocean" inside. She summons readers to their own interior spaces where Spirit may speak in words familiar, rich, and strange. Readers, having traveled the paths they opened, will return to explore again.

—Marilyn McEntyre
Author of *When Poets Pray*

I read *Song of the Selkie* with great pleasure. Jane Beal is a poet I admire, and these poems are wonderfully appealing: sensuous, deeply lyrical, joyous, filled with the spirit. I would recommend these poems to anyone.

—Jay Parini
Professor at Middlebury College
Author of *New and Collected Poems, 1975-2015*
and *Why Poetry Matters*

Other Books by Jane Beal

Poetry
Sanctuary
Songs from the Secret Life (recordings)
Made in the Image
Tidepools
Magical Poems for Girls
Magical Poems
Love-Song (also in recordings)
The Bird-Watcher's Diary Entries
Butterflies
Wild Birdsong
Epiphany: Birth Poems
A Pure Heart
Jazz Birding
Sunflower Songs
Roots of Apples
The Jazz Bird (recordings)
Rising: Poems for America
Spiritual Aviary for the Year, Vol. 1, 2, & 3
Transfiguration: A Midwife's Birth Poems
After the Labyrinth
Uncaged
Journey
Praise and Lament: Psalms for the God of Birds
Garden
Hail, Radiant Star!: Seven Medievalist Poets (poetry anthology)

Fiction
Eight Stories from Undiscovered Countries

Literary and Cultural Studies
John Trevisa and the English Polychronicon
Translating the Past: Essays on Medieval Literature
Illuminating Moses: A History of Reception
The Signifying Power of Pearl
Approaches to Teaching the Middle English Pearl
Pearl: A Middle English Edition and Modern English Translation
Illuminating Jesus in the Middle Ages

Song of the Selkie

Jane Beal

Aubade Publishing
Ashburn, VA

Copyright © 2020 Jane Beal

All rights reserved. No part of this publication may be reproduced, stored in a retrieval system, or transmitted in any form or by any means, electronic, mechanical, photocopying, recording, or otherwise, without the prior written permission of Aubade Publishing.

Edited by Joe Puckett

Cover, book design, and cover illustration by Cosette Puckett

Cover photo by Annie Flynn

Interior illustration by Emma Puckett

Library of Congress Control Number: 2020930698

ISBN: 978-1-951547-00-4

Published by Aubade Publishing, Ashburn, VA

Printed in the United States of America

For Josh

*in memory of
the music*

Late, by myself, in the boat of myself,
no light and no land anywhere,
cloud-cover thick. I try to stay
just above the surface, yet I'm already under
and living within the ocean.

>   —Rumi, translated by John
>   Moyne and Coleman Barks

Deep calls to deep in the roar of your waterfalls;
all your waves and breakers have swept over me.

>   —Psalm 42:7

*"Woe is me! Ah, woe is me!
I have seven bairns on land,
and seven in the sea."*

It is said that the man was brokenhearted about this. Whenever he rowed out fishing afterward, the seal would often swim round and round the boat, and it looked as if tears were running from its eyes.

>   —Joanna Cole, from "The
>   Seal's Skin," *Best Loved
>   Folktales of the World*

Preface

This collection of poems is one continuous series. In it, the reader will hear the voice of a Celtic selkie and the voices of others she imagines: the biblical Ruth and Jesus, a lighthouse keeper and a baby, a beloved widow, a young friend, and an old friend.

Inspiration for these poems came from diverse sources: the legend of the selkie and the biblical book of Ruth; studies of medieval *mappaemundi*, especially the one in Baudri of Bourgueil's poem "To Adela," which depicts the world map under a glass floor; the related idea of a dance floor between heaven and earth portrayed in the song "We Never Danced" by Neil Young and Crazy Horse, performed by the Motels, for the film *Made in Heaven*; Stephen King's *Firestarter* and the times my sisters Annie and Debbie helped me with aloe vera when I was burned; Joseph Bentz's take on Thomas Wolfe's *Look Homeward, Angel;* the medieval Persian poet and Sufi mystic Rumi; one of Josh Anway's Instagram video clips; the memorial service for Augustine Vegas at Church on the Hill in Vallejo, California; J.R.R. Tolkien's short story, "Smith of Wootten Major"; a tree in Willowcreek Park in Davis, CA; Saint Peter's Chapel on Mare Island; the medieval conception of the ladder of contemplation and the rungs of humility, illumination, purification, and unification with God; and the song "Golden Summer" by Songs of Water.

Acknowledgements

Thanks to editor Dr. John Han, "The Life" appears in *Integrité: A Journal of Faith and Learning*. Thanks to Dylan Freni, "Selkie Takes her Turn" appears in *Forgotten*. Thanks to Catherine Ghosh, "Selkie Finds the Sea" appears in *Journey of the Heart: Women's Spiritual Poetry*. Thanks to Dr. Pradeep Chaswal, "The Ladder of Contemplation" appears in *Literature Today*. Thanks to Patricia Caspars, "Untethered" appears in *West Trestle Review*. "The Enchanting Song" appears as "Song of the Selkie" in *Aji Magazine*. Thanks to Lora Zill, "Ruth and Ruah" appears in *A Time of Singing*.

Table of Contents

Song from the Sea	1
Jazz on Wednesday	2
The Life	4
Destiny	5
Before Reading the Book of Ruth	7
Selkie Counts the Cost	8
Like Water, Like Sky	10
Mappamundi	12
Conversation with a Friend in Colorado	13
Upon Sitting Down to Read the Book of Ruth Once Again	16
Question	18
Not Drowning	19
The Process	21
The Burned Hand	22
Becoming Ruth	25
Selkie and Ruth Have a Conversation	26
Cutting Open the Lemon	29
Stone Angel	30
Sometimes I am Selkie	31
Sometimes Ruth	32
The Enchanting Song	33
Expectation	36
Another Question	37
Untethered	38
A Train to the Sea	39
Selkie Takes Her Turn	40
I Saw a Widow Weeping	41
Twice	42
The Lighthouse Keeper in Chicago	43
The Flower That Never Fades	44
Ruth Gets Married Again	45
Flowers for the Wedding	47
Kyrie Eleison	48

Table of Contents

The Tree	49
Ruth and Ruah	50
Selkie in Saint Peter's Chapel	51
The Lighthouse Keeper Speaks	53
The Ladder of Contemplation	54
Illumination	55
Purity	56
After Years	57
Genealogy	58
A Vision of the Future	59
Selkie Finds the Sea	60
The Baby Gets the Last Word	61

Postscript Poems   63

Light and Water	65
Seashell	66
Into the Picture	67

Song of the Selkie

Song from the Sea

Selkie, selkie, singing—
she goes down deep into the sea:

she raises her head, laughing above
the white-crested waves,
so nothing is lost,

not even memory.

Jazz on Wednesday

If you want to be a choir director,
I understand:
        but I should tell you,
I was born to play jazz

to sing with someone who wants
to make music that has never been
heard before, *spontaneously*, music that rises
and falls from the soul, not the brain,
coming from our fingers and our throats

and exploding like a firecracker
in our hands, but without burning—

this music *shines!*

Even now, I know you
don't want to keep the music
        all contained,
something only written on a page—

to stand up with a thin baton in a concert hall
when we could jam all night long in the street,
when the sounds of our breathing could merge and join
in a present beyond beauty, beyond words,
beyond stars like glittering diamonds
        spangled across a midnight sky—

but if we don't sing together, if we don't play
anymore, ever after, I'll remember, I won't forget
and my love won't twist
what it once tried to hold, but take the rope
that won't support my weight, climbing the cliff—

take that rope, and unbind it, take the thin fibers
and lay them on this, my recycled skin,
one line after another, until there are five:

> *I'll fill in the spaces with the notes*
>
> *I heard you sing in the light,*
>
> *and then pick up my flute and play*
>
> *something that isn't written—*
>
> *the unspeakable jazz of the heart.*

The Life

I open my hands.
The butterfly lifts into the sky.
I have never seen
something so beautiful—
the life
        that goes
                toward heaven.

Destiny

I feel
blown away
like a dry leaf.

Now the rain begins
to fall

on my crackling
skin, so that it softens,
and I cling to the loam
dark as night
beneath me.

I feel
myself
disintegrating,
becoming one with the dirt,
sinking into the earth.

I feel the tender, slender roots
from a nearby patch of grass
reaching into me—

I feel
a dandelion seed.

What will we become,
this tiny seed and me,
entwining in the dark
under the earth
where no one else can see?

When the rain stops,
when my former shape
is unrecognizable,
when I am spread out
and taken in,

when I can't speak
in the usual way, when the vocal-chord veins
in my skin can't be played
like a harp, by the wind, the wind I love,
the wind I remember so well,

when I grow
through the new life
of a flower
pushing herself
through the soil to the sun,

opening her green self
to become her yellow self,
feeling the light
to transform into her white self,
clean and pure—

who will I be?
Will the wind come back
and blow through me,
scattering me again,
for the sake of someone else's wish?

Before Reading the Book of Ruth

Before reading the book of Ruth, I was sitting in silence: I saw myself, naked, standing under a waterfall. Bright water was pouring over me.

I looked into the water, and a silver fish leaped up! I caught this fish in my hands. It lay breathing between my palms, one eye looking at me. I let it go, back into the water, and I followed it downward.

Underwater, I found the bed of the stream. There were sparkling-bright jewels lying on the surface of the sandy streambed. I was transformed into a selkie as I was swimming over those gems, my eyes full of light, my lungs full of water, the lower half of my body like the lower half of a powerful seal—full of hidden meaning.

I sat down underwater, curling my tail around me, the upper half of my body floating in the gentle current as I opened the book that appeared between my hands. The pages were wet, of course, but they were not damaged at all. From the pages of the open book, jewels floated upward, hovering in the water before me,

bright and shining.

Selkie Counts the Cost

My song cost me something.
What did yours
cost you?

Did you give up your home
to walk on the sand?
Did you surrender
your white coat
to a strange man?

Did he take it, to keep it,
to lock it away
in a wooden chest
you couldn't find,
closed with a golden key
he never left behind?

Were your children half-breeds,
distorted by desire,
longing for your love,
longing for the sea,
longing for a true union
between their parents
that never could be?

O, take me deep,
back into the wave,
so I can swim like I was meant to be,
like my life was meant to be.

If I hear my children crying,
I will come back to the shore,
and play with them in the shallow water,
as if the lies and the imprisonment
don't matter anymore.

And if I see you, Man,
standing at the top of that tall lighthouse,
I will dive back down into my Mystery—
my dark, my splendid, my endlessly flowing sea.

It's true: this song cost me more than I knew.
On the day after tomorrow,
what will it cost you?

I will hold a shell to your ear,
and in the end, you will not hear a sound
even though the wine-dark sea
is very near.

Before you,
    there was another.

Like Water, Like Sky

I am dancing
when you appear before me.
I reach up
and touch your face.
I step close to you,
into your embrace.
I feel your arms
around me.

I feel this ancient love.

My face against your face,
breathing in, breathing
out, my lips
brushing the line of your jaw,
while my right hand
drifts up along your neck
to hold your head
and feel your hair,
to feel you.

You are so near to me.

I feel your hands,
on my shoulder blades,
then my back,
now my hips,
pulling me closer
to you, feeling this,
our two bodies
together.

It seems impossible, but it's real.

This, my touch,
this, our ancient love,
remembered and being
renewed by hope
even across a vast distance,
even from far away,
even without opening our mouths,
you and me, bodies like song—

singing!

I can be your harmony,
as you are
my sweetest melody,
and we are
gently entwining
like wind around a runner,
like waves around a swimmer
pushing out from shore
into the deep water.

Look at me, lover.

I step back, but only a little.
I want to see your face.
See my face, too.
Your eyes, that color,
the color of dark water
with flecks of gold.
Now see my eyes, too,
blue and gray and green—

like water, like sky.

Mappamundi

With my bright-blue eye, I spy
a world map in the sky:
I take it down
and wrap it around
my baby, my baby.

In my arms,
   you have ten thousand charms.

Conversation with a Friend in Colorado

I know you went out
to rewire four hundred solar panels
in a field near Golden.
The snow-capped Rockies
were shining in the West.

When you told me
you had been there, I knew
your hands were cold,
and I sent you a fire
from California to warm them.

I sent you my memories
of riding a Ferris wheel
high over the town
of Santiago de Compostela
in España.

I sent you a pile of medieval maps,
a classic merry-go-round,
a painter's palate, a dancer in red,
roofing in the summertime, fireworks,
a picture of myself, listening to you.

I sent you a tiny kiss, a wish,
the idea of bird-watching
because birds are so free when they fly,
a Steller's jay, high in the mountains,
a golden heart, a real smile, a falling star.

You sent me *beautiful*,
you sent me your smile,
you sent me your eyes
with your heart shining in them,
you sent me your day.

You sent me Colorado,
the sunlight bright on the snow,
American Pickers, ancient aliens, and history,
you sent me not being scared
and sharing whatever you feel.

You sent me *thought of you earlier*,
and *maybe one day we can do that together*
—watch the birds, ride a Ferris wheel—
and *I enjoy you*
and *are you going to bed*?

I never expected this—
your words in my mind
in the silence, despite the distance,
or the yearning that I feel
to see you and hold you in my arms.

I never expected my body
to answer your body,
I never expected to feel
such a strong desire, a desire
for you.

I don't know what's right
or what's wise, and that frightens me.
I've known you for years,
but I never knew what you felt,
and even now, I wonder how it can be true.
Is there a tower we can climb
together? Is there a place we could find
in each other's lives? I want to look out
from a height with you by my side,
and I want to feel you near me.

O God, what will it take
to know what's true
and experience love and joy
on this earth
and in my anguished life?

Upon Sitting Down to Read the Book of Ruth Once Again

I was climbing the golden stairs, dressed in a white toga like a Greek girl from a Maxfield Parrish painting. The light shone around me like midmorning.

At the top of the stairs, to my left, was a green plant growing out of a large pot. I bent my head toward it, toward the scent of a large pink flower. I took the flower in the open palms of my two hands. As I did so, a giant gust of wind blew open the doors to the Temple!

I walked in, as if I had been invited, putting the pink flower in my hair. In the Temple were white columns on either side of me, straight and tall in the dark. At the front was a blue fire in the shape of a circle. The Fourth Man stepped out of it, and came to me, and called me: *Ruth.*

We turned together. I looked out of the Temple doors behind me toward the horizon. I saw the Sun was rising, rising and filling the world with light. I saw stars glimmering around that great light, and I wondered how the Sun could shine, but the stars still be seen, too. Then I saw the moon, joined to the Sun, an eclipse of beauty:

*the light of day, the light of night,
joined by the singing stars
encircling them like a crown—*

*a man and a woman in love
and their children
    like diamonds
        in the sky.*

Question

How do You know
how to go

in-between
stories?

Not Drowning

I was in-between transformations,
half woman, half seal, weeping
and clinging to a stone in the sea
as the waves rushed over me,
pushing me forward, pulling me back.

I held on, but my cheek was lacerated
by the barnacles on the stone.
I kept crying, and I could not let go.
My eyes were closed.
My face was bleeding.

Somehow, after a time, I released my hold,
and I sank back into the waves.
I turned myself downward,
becoming my underwater self,
propelling myself deep into the Mystery.

There was a heart hanging in the sea,
shaped of bright jewels,
and I swam through it,
so that it became my necklace,
and I rose to the surface of the water.

I broke the surface, breathing, half woman
once again, breathing in and
breathing out, deep breaths that raised my breasts
in the water, eyes closed, moonlight
shining on me, white and pure.

A wooden door was floating in the water,
and I cast my arms over it, clinging to it,
between transformations again,
half woman resting in the world of air,
my seal self still treading water.

My face was against the rough wood,
like it had been against the stone.
I was no longer bleeding, but my eyes
were still closed, my tears thick
underneath my eyelids.

I felt that he was there. I opened
my eyes, and I looked at him,
shadowy on the other side of the door,
half in and half out of the water with me,
and I wondered who he was.

Then he reached out his hand,
and he rested it on my head,
and I knew him: the Fourth Man,
out of the fire, into the water,
near me, loving me, comforting

my soul.

The Process

Is the earth young?
Is the earth old?
There's so much more
in the depths of the earth
than silver and gold.

Let's read the sedimentary rocks
and ask what their layers mean:
let's interpret the Grand Canyon
and the Colorado River
and the past that no one has seen.

If we do not know,
we can guess:
if we lose ourselves
in the asking, at least
we discover the process.

The Burned Hand

I.

"The burned hand teaches best—about fire," the Philologist said, and he was right.

I used to burn myself all the time. Not on purpose. It's just that I wasn't paying attention in the kitchen. I was unaware of my body, unaware of pots and pans that were scorching hot. My sister finally prayed for me—that this would stop.

Did you know that if you fry your fingers on the metal of a hot pot or pan, and then quickly remove them from where they have made contact with the metal, the skin will continue to burn?

It will continue to burn.

The heat is already inside of the flesh. It's cooking like meat. But this is your hand—your fingers—your fingertips. There is no candle that shines like that invisible pain.

II.

I know what that pain feels like. The pain that makes you scream, and drop the pot—that's the first few seconds. But the burn doesn't stop then. It keeps going, relentless, no matter how much aloe vera you smear on it. Aloe vera helps, though. It does help.

I need aloe vera for my brain, where every thought of you is a blistering burn, burning me. Not with desire, like Dido in the *Aeneid*. More like that little girl, the raging Firestarter, in that book by Stephen King.

More like that little girl.

I know you have no idea what I mean.

III.

I'm sorry. I'm so sorry that I want the flame you lit to warm my hands to explode like a match set to a tank of gasoline. I want you to feel what it feels like to be a burn victim. But that's not your destiny. It's mine.

Only because you are a liar, like other liars I have known, and because you took something from me. You are a thief and a liar. I treated you with honor. You treated me with shame. You only used what you wanted from me, and when you got more of what you wanted somewhere else, you leveled what I had built without hesitation.

Jesus was crucified beside a good thief and that other one. Which one are you? And if it had been a woman up there, what would she have said?

> *I want to forgive you.*
> *Please take away my pain.*

No one knows me. No one hears me. No one sees me. There is no candle that shines like this invisible pain.

I didn't know I was this angry. I know it's pointless to feel this way. Better to forgive, better to forget. Better to ask my sister for pure aloe vera.

Pure. Aloe. Vera.

Becoming Ruth

I was walking in a shallow river. The tendril of an underwater plant circled around my left ankle. I strode forward, and it released me.

Then I began to rise.

Above the water, into the air, spinning round and round in a gyre, through white clouds shot through with sunlight, I was rising. The light! The light! Past the atmosphere of earth, higher and higher, I rose past the sphere of the Moon—until I reached another dimension of existence.

In that high and rarified place, there is a glass floor. Beneath it, the earth is laid out like a green and blue *mappmamundi*. I had glass slippers on my feet like a princess, and the Prince, to whom we are all pearls, came to dance with me.

We were dancing across the glass floor, and the glass slipper on my left foot struck the floor. As it did, sparks flew up from the heel of my shoe like it was a flint rock. Like a flint rock, my dancing shoes made tiny fires in heaven.

If you look up at night,
       you'll see those sparks.

              They're stars.

Selkie and Ruth Have a Conversation

Yes, where I come from, women draw the water from the wells, but when I went to work in the field of my future husband—I didn't know I was going to marry him, then, that day—but he had the young men working for him drawing the water for us, the women!

Really?

Really. And my first husband's name meant "weakling," but my second husband's name meant "strength." Isn't that interesting?

Yes, it is.

Have you ever been married?

Yes. I was married once. I transformed into a woman, and I walked upon the shore, and a man from the shore took my coat from me. Then I could not transform back into the underwater creature I know so well how to be. I had children with him, but I longed to go back into the deep places, back down into the extraordinary Mystery.

I didn't have any children with my first husband, but I did have one with my second: a son. We named him Obed. My mother-in-law— my first husband's mother, actually—suckled him at her own breasts! Isn't that amazing? She loved our son that much.

I left my children with their father. When I found my husband's key, when I found the treasure chest where he had locked up my coat, I unlocked that chest, and I took back what he had stolen from me so I could be free.

But I don't feel free. I feel half-woman, half-creature. I don't breathe right underwater anymore. I don't breathe right in the air. I want my children in my arms when I don't have any, and when I do, they ache from the endless emptiness.

The man is looking for me. I see him, sometimes, in the lighthouse. But he doesn't see me in the waves. I can hide from the light. The darkness is my only companion.

Selkie?

Yes, Ruth?

You know that you can make choices that change the end of your story, don't you? I walked fifty miles and crossed two rivers to leave my home and enter the House of Bread. When my mother-in-law and I were starving, I went out to glean in the field. I could have stayed home. I could have turned back. Instead, I gave birth to the future.

I have given birth to the future, too. My children are growing up on land. It's just that I want them to be able to transform like I can. I want them to see the wondrous Kingdom of the Sea. I want not to be divided between the sea and the shore.

Do you know that I keep getting stuck between my two selves, half one, half the other? I feel so strange. Sailors call me mermaid, *but when I hear them, I go back down into the deep places.*

The deep places are always calling me.

Cutting Open the Lemon

I cut open
   the lemon

only to see
   the knife

had split
   the seed.

Stone Angel

A man carved a stone angel
and set it by his door:
at times she looked into the house,
and at times she looked out
for something more.

The man had a young son
who wandered in the perilous realm:
the boy was easily lost,
alas, to his cost
but his mind was bright-under-helm.

One night, in the dark, far
from his friends in town,
he dreamed that the angel
opened her stone wings
and wore a golden crown.

Her wings opened white!
Her face was alight!
Her eyes were as blue
as a stormy sea, and as true,
in the dream he dreamed at midnight.

Wake up, O sleeper,
she whispered, *and rise
from the dead—
for the new life is waiting
and the new sunrise.*

Sometimes I am Selkie

Sometimes I am Selkie,
thrashing in the waves—

looking to the Lighthouse
at the man looking down for me.

O fear!

I fear to see him up there dancing
with someone who always lived on land—

someone who doesn't dream underwater
or hide her pearls in sand.

I fear to look too closely,
I fear to look away,
I fear to hope for something good,
I fear him coming back for me one fine day.

In all my life, I never knew
an undying, unfailing love.

In all my life, I never knew
a love that conquered fear.

O fear!

If I could be free, I would be free
to live and love and choose—

if I could be free, I would be free,
no matter how much I might lose.

Sometimes Ruth

The mockingbird flew on an arc of light
across a waterfall to a tree:

in its branches, he transformed
into the Man Whose Arms Are Wings.

I climbed the tree and laid my head
against his chest and heard his heart

and he, for his part, spread his wings over me
and held me close in his embrace.

The Enchanting Song

— in memory of Augustine Vegas

I am a singer, and I must sing:
that is what few people understand.
Whether in love or death,
I must sing the enchanting song
that draws listeners closer to me.

You don't know how many men
I have seen drowned in the deep of the Deep,
the sailors we tried to rescue
as the water filled up their lungs
and they, and their ships, sank to the floor of the sea.

Some wrapped their arms around our necks,
and we swam with them to the surface,
so that they breathed, and lived, and went back to shore
where they told the truth about us and our songs—
the selkies who saved them from storms.

Some told lies. They said that we sang
the enchanting song, a serenade of death,
and filled them with desire to plunge into the flood,
to seek love and death and oblivion in our arms—
like sea witches, like goddesses or shee demons.

How little those liars know! What have they seen,
under the waves, of the faces of the pale dead?
The swollen eyes, fully dilated and black,
the mouths open and expressions distorted,
the arms and legs floating, helpless, without strength?

You don't know why I sing. You don't know who I have
saved from drowning—or who I couldn't save.
You never transformed your true self into the image
of one who died, a pregnant woman who flung herself
from the starboard side of an ancient wooden ship

in despair from her pain, to give birth to a dead child,
in the sea, and you don't know how we carried her
back to the surface, and her baby to an invisible grave
in the heart of the sea, in my heart forever, the stillborn,
and her mother, crying, until she finally stopped.

You never became one of the lost ones
to try to deal with your grief, the incomprehensible
sorrow of watching someone die, before your eyes,
as their pupils open and yours narrow
in the dark beneath the Deep.

You never walked upon the shore, human for the first time,
or wondered about the love of a man in a lighthouse,
who tries to save the ships by guiding them home
with a beacon to declare the source of safety—
you never thought he might understand.

You never went back from the shore to the sea,
knowing that a man in a lighthouse
is different from a selkie, from a woman water creature
who saves men in the sea, who brings the dying
to the surface to breathe.

You never rocked in the cradle of the loving waves
and watched from their embrace as a pirate
held a pistol to the heart of a prince, and pulled the trigger,
so that the prince fell, already dead, blood flowing
from his chest into the sea.

I am a singer, and I must sing—
> *that is what few people understand.*

Expectation

The bees are in the lavender.
The dark butterfly is in the white blossoms
of the tall plum tree.

I step forward,
and a reddish-brown bird flies from the brush cover
to hide in the green leaves of the olive tree.

Yesterday's wind blew open the Spring.
Rain is expected on Wednesday.

Another Question

Are you and I going to be friends now,
Lighthouse Man? As Tevia says:

A bird may love a fish,
  but where will they live?

I don't know, but I hear you singing,
high up there, morning and night.

You sing low, you sing high,
and even when you cannot hear me,
I am singing with you.

Maybe when I cannot hear you,
you are still singing with me.

In the air above my head,
our voices meet.

Our words, without our bodies,
embrace one another.

This is a different kind of magic,
a different kind of child

being conceived now
in mid-air

like a dream
at dawn.

Untethered

From the waves, I watched
a little child on the shore
who walked up to a fishing boat
tied to a rock in the shallow part
of this cove—and untied it.

The boat drifted out,
away from the shore,
traveling farther and farther out to sea,
empty—without a soul inside of it—
toward an unknown horizon.

It was my child who did this.
It was my boat.

A Train to the Sea

A train rolls slowly down the track.
It's impossible to cross over right now.
But on the other side of the rolling train,
we see, through the gaps, two trees,
covered with tiny star-lights,
shining in the dark.

Will this train roll off the track,
across the sand and into the sea?
Will this train come down, deep down,
into the Deep for me?
Is there a golden ticket, a conductor to the shore,
a passenger, with your eyes,
calling me through an open door?

I think Ruth and her Strength are riding
on the top of this train.

Selkie Takes Her Turn

I remember being five years old on the playground,
standing in front of another child on a swing, and
counting, "One-one, two-two, three-three . . ."
all the way to ten, and then
shouting victoriously, "Off-off!"

The other child would slow down, and stop,
and give me a chance to swing
(there were only four swings
on my playground, you see),
and I would take my turn.

I would swing high, and point my toes
at the bright, blue California sky—
I would kick at the clouds, and I
would marvel at what it was like to be a girl,
a girl alone in a beautiful sky-world.

In the afternoon, I would walk home,
past the fountain in the square.
It was a long way home.
But I would slow down, and stop
by the pretty fountain, and remember

as the water splashed over the tiled mosaic
of Old World wishes and dreams:
I used to live in the water,
        and I was baptized in the sea
                before I was ever born again on land.

I Saw a Widow Weeping

I saw a widow weeping,
but when her friends embraced her,
I saw that she would laugh,
and I thought, in my world of silence:

*even in laughter, the heart may ache,
and joy may end in grief.*

Where is our Shalom?

Twice

I think everything is born twice:
the bee from the wax,
the butterfly from the wrap,
the selkie from the sea—

even the sorrow that comes
from deep inside of you
and deep inside of me.

Peace, Widow Woman—
my peace I give to you.

The Lighthouse Keeper in Chicago

The Lighthouse Keeper took a journey inland,
from the shore of the sea to Chicago—

from fog and rain and waves and wind
to snow and ice and darkness in the daytime.

There were songs in his heart
and thoughts in his mind.

When he looked up at the storm clouds,
he saw one that looked like a selkie.

When can I give you, I sing from the West,
the flower that never fades?

The Flower That Never Fades

Did you ever read the story of the little boy
who grew up to be a Blacksmith, but first acquired,

by chance or by design, a star passport
from our world into the perilous realm?

He wore it on his forehead, so he was called Starbrow
whenever he wandered in Faërie.

He danced with the queen of that country,
and she gave to him a flower that never fades—

> *a flower that never fades,*
> *a flower that never fades.*

That boy is my secret cousin. After his children
had the flower a long time, they gave it to me.

Now I am giving it to you, Lighthouse Keeper,
so you will know how much you are loved.

Ruth Gets Married Again

I trusted him, Selkie, I trusted
his integrity. That is why I went down
to the threshing floor anointed with perfume
and waited, watching him, as he threshed out the barley
and afterwards ate and drank and lay down.

Then I came quietly from the shadows
and lay down near him, still as I could be,
until he turned over in the night, utterly startled,
and noticed I was there! He asked, "Who are you?"
and I said, "I am your *amah*, Ruth."

I reminded him of the words he spoke to me
when we first met: he prayed that the Lord,
under whose wings I had taken refuge, would bless me.
So that night, I prayed that he would spread his own
wings over me, for he was a kinsman redeemer.

He blessed me a second time, for my kindness,
and he told me not to be afraid,
for if the man who, by right, could have redeemed
but didn't, still refused, then he said he would do
all that I asked of him.

He told me to lie down again, in the dark,
until day came, and I did, but I lay awake,
as the scent of my perfume rose over
the threshing floor, and I knew he was awake, too,
listening to my breathing.

In the morning, before the sun had risen,
he gave me six measures of grain,

and he walked to the city gate,
and settled the matter
that very day.

So we were married,
and no one in Bethlehem
can stop singing about it!

Flowers for the Wedding

I always wanted red roses
and dark-green ivy
and bright-white baby's breath
in my bouquet when I got married,
but now I know

I will add rue,
a yellow flower with blue leaves.

Kyrie Eleison

Will I be a thousand years old
before Jesus does this miracle?

Lord, have mercy.

The Tree

The tree has strewn
the white petals
of her blossoming flowers
across the ground
like a bridal veil.

Ruth and Ruah

The wind blew
and chaff from the threshed barley
swirled in the air
over the field

where I saw you, kinsman redeemer,
standing in sheaves still up standing,
dressed in blue and gold.

Selkie in Saint Peter's Chapel

Sometimes it's hard for me to put it together,
but I want to tell you: there was a baby.
He died, and I lost him. Underneath the tears
for every other person who has died and left my life,
there is that boy, who slipped from my body
with the blood. There are names for this, but I can't
say them. I sing songs, lullabies for the baby dead,
who lives somewhere else, apart from me.

I've seen him in heaven, a young child, perfect,
seven years old forever, and I have given him his name.
I've held him in my imaginary arms, and
we have ridden together on an elephant
across the desert, across the sands of Time,
and we've been together, beyond death, beyond life,
beyond memory, beyond hope. Beyond possible
and impossible, I have known my son.

Let me take you now into Saint Peter's Chapel
on Mare Island, where we can look up together and see
Jesus walking on the bluest water, light shining
behind him, as his arms reach down to us,
accepting all our sorrows, holding all the pain in our souls,
calling us out to be with him, where he won't let us
drown, in the deep waters, in the Deep,
in the Mystery of hope calling for love, real love.

Here, Michael holds a sword, and Gabriel a horn,
and Galahad kneels, illuminated in darkness,
across from the Good Shepherd, who is sitting

in a garden, and the flowers are all around him,
like the tiny white flowers that opened on the Third Day
of Creation, wondrous, and then were reflected,
in the night, by stars that appeared in the black sky, shining,
tiny, bright-white mirrors of earth's flowers, promising

even in the black ocean of the sky, there will be
Light. Yes, there is light. Let there be light:
let it be, let it be, let it be.

The Lighthouse Keeper Speaks

Someday, I am going to tell you
what you told me: we are clay in the Potter's hand.
If the pot is broken, he can remake it.
If it is shattered, he can take the shards and pieces,
and he can make you into something new,
a mosaic of beauty that testifies
to the true loving-kindness of God.

I love you, Selkie, I love you—
    broken and remade,
        I love you more than you know.

> *And he dreamed, and behold, there was a ladder set up on the earth, and the top of it reached to heaven. And behold, the angels of God were ascending and descending on it!*
>
> —Genesis 28:12

The Ladder of Contemplation

Sometimes the total madness of being human
makes me want to laugh and cry at the same time.
Like that acrobat girl I saw on a Cirque du Soleil stage
in San Francisco: surrounded by smiling performers,
she could not pretend.

The ladders on that stage reached into the heights
of the circus tent, and men and women climbed them,
only to jump down, dancing in mid-air,
or bicycling upside down, or flipping and spinning
and landing, feet-first, on the trampoline

and bouncing back, reaching out to catch the ropes
swinging above their heads, like angels
who used to have wings, and still remembered
how to fly. So they went surging up and
plunging down, then out of the abyss, back into heights.

If only rising on the ladder of contemplation
were as easy as humility, purity, and illumination.

Illumination

*I will shine my light upon you, Selkie,
and at last, you will see
the kingdom of God.*

Purity

O, Obed! My milk is in your mouth.
O my little son, your mouth is milk-wet
with my love for you.

How I love you, little one, little son—
  how I love you, tiny servant of God.

After Years

There was another man,
and he could have married me.
He had the greater right,
and his kinship was closer.
But he chose not to redeem.

It was a long summer in the fields.
The work never seemed to end.
I felt tired, and sometimes, angry.
Why would the one who could do this,
a good deed of loving-kindness—
why would he refuse?

On the day my Strength
called him out, that kinsman of ours
took off his own sandal,
and ceded his right to my love
forever.

It is impossible to be angry now.
The sadness of that disappointed hope
flows away like water and evaporates
in the desert. When I think of that man,
I think of John the Baptist.
Why would he refuse?

The Baptist said he was not worthy
to untie the sandal of the Bridegroom.
He cried: *Behold!* And he pointed the way
toward the pure Lamb of God
who takes away the sin of the world.

Genealogy

All the names in the line of descent,
seed to seed, are less important
than this truth: I am the grandmother
of a king, and the great-grandmother
of the Messiah.

Listen to my life.

A Vision of the Future

I sat down in the Presence.
I opened my heart.
I listened to the voice of the Holy One.

I closed my eyes, and—*suddenly!*—
I could see, you and me,
and I was dressed in white,
and you were dressed in black,
and we were dancing!

I opened my eyes in surprise!
The Lord told me
to close them again.

I saw the two of us, sitting side by side,
and you lay your hand on my belly,
and our baby was inside of me.

Again, again, I heard it!
A baby's first birth-cry.
I had given birth to our son.
I held him in my arms,
and I looked into his yes,
and darling, they were your eyes:
bright blue.

Then the Lord said to me:
watch what I will do.

And tears sprang into my eyes!

Selkie Finds the Sea

I went into the desert with my lover.
He was carrying a cobalt-blue wine bottle
in one hand. We reached a place
where we stopped: there was nothing
but golden sand, as far as the eye could see,
and the sun was hot and bright.

My lover is a magician—a good one,
an artist. He uncorked the wine bottle,
and do you know what was inside?

The Ocean!

My ocean, my deep, deep Ocean,
my Mystery was inside, and he poured it out,
and I was laughing for joy!

I ran to the waves like a child,
and plunged into their beloved embrace,
but I remained a woman, a beautiful woman,
as whole as the day as I was born,
as pure as rain in the North,
as true as a bright-white star in the sky.

When my lover saw that I did not change,
he came into the waves with me,
and he embraced me in my arms.

O, how I love you, Selkie-girl—
    I love how you are.

The Baby Gets the Last Word

I'm glad you figured it out.
Now, I will live.

Postscript Poems

Light and Water

Light on the water,
deep water shimmering on the surface—

and the light goes down
into the well of love.

Everything is illuminated.

The hidden treasures, the lost seashells,
the songs water creatures sing,

the ripple effect of your skipping stone
sinking down to the sand.

Everything is illuminated.

Do you know what water lilies
look like from underneath?

Do you know how to breathe
in the deep places?

Everything is illuminated.

Touch the roots of flowers
that float on the water.

See what can be seen.
Hear me.

Seashell

I was sitting
on the sand.

A wave curled around me
without touching me.

When the water receded,
there was a small seashell

—a brown-and-white conch shell—
on the sand next to me.

I looked up then, and I saw you walking
across the sand to me.

You came close
and sat down beside me.

I was leaning against you.
Our bodies were touching.

I picked up the shell in my hand.
We were looking at it together.

When I turned it over, in my palm,
I saw something astonishing:

there were diamonds
inside of it!

When I opened my eyes,
I heard the voice of God.

Into the Picture

I was semi-sitting in a blank space
wearing bluish-white and gray.

You came into the picture
with your bright red hair.

You sat down next to me,
and gradually, we got closer together.

When I lay down
my belly was visible.

You set a mound of dark dirt on it,
and there was a single yellow flower in the dirt.

The flower head spun around, and
circular white lights sprang out from it!

Then birds, blue birds, emerged, too,
and they were singing above us—

swooping in a circle,
singing.

*Tell me the meaning
of this parable.*

Afterword

In English, "ruth" means *sorrow*. In Hebrew, "ruth" means *friend*. Ruth is also a book in the Bible; it tells the story of a woman named Ruth, a widow who left her own country to travel to Bethlehem, in Judah, with her mother-in-law, Naomi, where she worked in the fields to support both of them. There she met Boaz, who is called a "gibbor hayil," a very worthy man. They later married, and had a son, named Obed, who is believed by many to be the ancestor of David and, centuries later, Jesus.

"Ruth" also means *compassion*. When one person has compassion for another, she suffers with that person. Ruth suffered death, loss, a long journey, hard work, and poverty with Naomi because she loved her. Whenever we suffer with another person, in a sense, we become like Ruth.

"Ruth" has a third meaning: *regret, remorse,* or even *contrition* and *repentance*. It is a deeply heartfelt emotion that can move a person to want to change and, then, to choose to change. This is the rarest sense of the word.

The word "ruth" entered the English language between the years 1125–1175. It is related to the verb "to rue," which means "to feel sorrow," "to repent," and "to bitterly regret." Someone who rues a deed intensely wishes that it had never happened, that the event that caused the feeling had never occurred. Apparently—along the same line as "true/truth"— a "th" was appended to "rue," leaving us with "rue/ruth." "Rue" derives from an Old English verb, but the noun "ruth" may be influenced by the Old Norse word, *hryggð*, which, again, means *sorrow*.

While the nominative form "ruth" developed from the verbal form "rue," the word "rue" can also be a noun with another meaning: a yellow flower with bluish leaves, one that gives off a strong scent. Medicinal herbals from the Middle Ages asserted that it sharpened eyesight. In some cultures, such as Greece and Ethiopia, it is used in cuisine, but the bitter taste of its leaves associated it (in English poetry) with the traditional meanings of "ruth": sorrow and bitter regret. Two of Shakespeare's female characters— Perdita from *The Winter's Tale* and Ophelia from *Hamlet*— give the rue flower to others in moments of grief or madness. But Shakespeare also called it "th' herb of grace" (*Richard III* III.iv.105). In Lithuania, brides traditionally wear rue on their wedding day. There, the flower is a symbol of purity.

All of these aspects of the word "ruth" are easy to understand. What is not easy to do, however, is to find a picture or a story that represents the experience of *becoming ruth*. But I found one: the song of the selkie.

In Irish, Scandinavian, and Native folklore, the selkie is a magical creature who has the form of a seal in water, but the form of a human on land. Sometimes selkie women come out of the sea, shed their seal coats and become human just to dance on the shore. In one myth, a man takes a selkie's coat so she cannot transform back into her sea self. She is forced to be his wife, they have children, and live together for a long time. But one day, she finds the key to the chest where her husband has locked away her coat. She takes it back, and flees to the water, abandoning her husband and children in order to go home, be herself, and be free.

In another myth, the selkie wife truly loves her husband, and only transforms into her seal self to save his life when he is caught in a storm at sea. She cannot become a woman again, so although the man's life is saved, the love relationship is lost. The love itself, of course, remains.

In general, selkie legends are tragic stories of love and loss and, of course, magic. They have captured the modern imagination in two films: "The Secret of Roan Inish" (1994) and "Song of the Sea" (2014). There is a version of the selkie story from Iceland, "#86 The Seal's Skin," included in Joanna Cole's *Best Loved Folktales of the World* (1982).

Selkie women are a bit like mermaids. It is certainly possible to imagine a half-transformed selkie as a mermaid. Both selkies and mermaids can be beautiful and alluring, and their voices are enchanting. But Irish selkies are not Disney's "Little Mermaid" nor are they Greek sirens. They are not simple fairy stories with happy endings intended to entertain children. Nor are they Homeric horrors calling men to their deaths: selkies are the ones saving men from death.

Selkies give us a perfect picture of what it feels like to be caught between two worlds, becoming a man's friend and yet feeling the deep sorrow of the loss of another world that he does not know as she does, even if he is a sailor on stormy seas or a lighthouse keeper on the shore.

The poems in this collection give voice to that experience. I hope they will resonate with my readers.

Jane Beal
La Verne, CA
March 2019

About the Author

Dr. Jane Beal is a poet. She was born and raised in northern California, where she received her BA (Sonoma State University), MA (Sonoma State University), and PhD (UC Davis) in English literature with concentrations in biblical, classical, and medieval literature. She also holds a Certificate in Midwifery from Mercy in Action College of Midwifery. She has served as a professor at Wheaton College, Colorado Christian University, and the University of California, Davis, teaching literature and creative writing, and as a midwife in the United States, Uganda, and the Philippine Islands. She now teaches at the University of La Verne in southern California.

In addition to *Song of the Selkie: Becoming Ruth*, she is the author of other poetry collections, including *Sanctuary* (Finishing Line Press, 2008), *Rising: Poems for America* (Wipf and Stock, 2015) and *Journey* and *Garden* (Origami Poems, 2019) as well as several more published by Lulu Press: *Made in the Image*, *Magical Poems*, *Tidepools*, *Love-Song*, *Butterflies*, *Epiphany: Birth Poems*, *A Pure Heart*, *Sunflower Songs*, *The Roots of Apples*, *Transfiguration: A Midwife's Birth Poems*, *Uncaged* and *Praise and Lament: Psalms for the God of Birds* as well as her Birdwatcher Trilogy, *The Bird-Watcher's Diary Entries*, *Wild Birdsong*, and *Jazz Birding*. She has made three recording projects, *Songs from the Secret Life*, *Love-Song*, and, with her brother, saxophonist and composer Andrew Beal, *The Jazz Bird*. She also writes fiction, creative non-fiction, literary criticism, and music.

To learn more, visit **janebeal.wordpress.com**.

Here is love, vast as the ocean,
Lovingkindness as the flood,
When the Prince of Life, our Ransom,
Shed for us His precious blood.

—William Rees,
"Here is Love"

www.ingramcontent.com/pod-product-compliance
Lightning Source LLC
Chambersburg PA
CBHW052118110526
44592CB00013B/1664